How to Draw the Life and Times of

William Jefferson Clinton

Miriam J. Gross

The Rosen Publishing Group's
PowerKids Press™
New York

For Martin.

Published in 2006 by The Rosen Publishing Group, Inc.
29 East 21st Street, New York, NY 10010

First Edition

Editor: Daryl Heller
Book Design: Gregory Tucker

Illustrations: All illustrations by Albert Hanner.
Photo Credits: p. 4 Courtesy Georgetown University; p. 7 © Wally McNamee/Corbis; p. 8 Courtesy Arkansas Deptartment of Parks and Tourism; p. 9, 20 © Getty Images; p. 10 (top) © Arnie Sachs/Corbis; p. 10 (bottom) © Lebrecht Music and Arts Photo Library/Alamy; p. 12 © Oxford Picture Library/Alamy; p. 16 © Brooks Kraft/Corbis; p. 18 (top) © Joseph Sohm/ChromoSohm Inc./Corbis; p. 18 (bottom) © AP/Wide World Photos; p. 24 © 2002 GeoAtlas; p. 26 Courtesy Dr. Mark Dimmitt, Arizona-Sonora Desert Museum; p. 28 © Bettmann/Corbis.

Library of Congress Cataloging-in-Publication Data

Gross, Miriam J.
    How to draw the life and times of William Jefferson Clinton / Miriam J. Gross.— 1st ed.
        p. cm. — (A kid's guide to drawing the presidents of the United States of America)
    Includes index.
    ISBN 1-4042-3018-1 (library binding)
    1. Clinton, Bill, 1946– —Juvenile literature. 2. Presidents—United States—Biography—Juvenile literature. 3. Drawing—Technique—Juvenile literature. I. Title. II. Series.
    E886.G76 2006
    973.929092—dc22
                                    2005027850

Printed in China

Contents

Meet William Jefferson Clinton

William Jefferson Clinton became the forty-second president of the United States in 1993. He is also known as Bill Clinton. During his eight years in office, Clinton tried to increase access to education and health care for all America's citizens. He also strengthened the

nation's economy. As president Clinton encouraged peace between warring countries in Europe and the Middle East.

Bill Clinton grew up in Arkansas, one of the poorest states in America. His father, William Jefferson Blythe Jr., died before Clinton was born. Clinton's mother, Virginia Cassidy Blythe, raised her son with the help of her parents. When Clinton was four years old, his mother married a car salesman named Roger Clinton.

Clinton attended school in Hot Springs, Arkansas, where he made excellent grades. In the 1950s and 1960s, when Clinton was growing up, southern states such as Arkansas were segregated. Clinton was upset by the unfair treatment he witnessed toward African Americans. The leaders of the civil rights movement, who sought to end segregation, inspired Clinton. Hoping that he, too, could make a difference to his country, Clinton studied politics and law in college. In 1978, he was elected governor of Arkansas, where he committed himself to improving public education for the children of his home state.

You will need the following supplies to draw the life and times of William Jefferson Clinton:

✓ A sketch pad   ✓ An eraser   ✓ A pencil   ✓ A ruler

These are some of the shapes and drawing terms you need to know:

Horizontal Line	——	Squiggly Line	∿
Oval	⬭	Trapezoid	⏢
Rectangle	▭	Triangle	△
Shading		Vertical Line	│
Slanted Line	/	Wavy Line	∿

The Presidency

When Bill Clinton became president in 1993, the United States' two main political parties, the Democrats and the Republicans, were having trouble working together. Many Democrats believed that the government should provide opportunities to the poor through programs such as welfare. In contrast many Republicans believed the government should play a smaller part in such issues and work toward creating a strong economy. Clinton called himself a New Democrat. He hoped to bridge the two parties by limiting government assistance while making it easier for poor people to get jobs.

During a time when his own country was so divided, Clinton played an important part in encouraging peace talks between foreign leaders. In Oslo, Norway, in 1993, Clinton supported peace talks between Israel and Palestine. In 1998, he worked with leaders of Great Britain, Ireland, and Northern Ireland to help bring peace between religious groups in Northern Ireland.

President Clinton is shown here in 1993 with Palestinian leader Yasser Arafat (right) and Israeli prime minister Yitzhak Rabin. The three world leaders met in the White House to sign a peace treaty called the Israel-PLO Agreement.

Bill Clinton's Arkansas

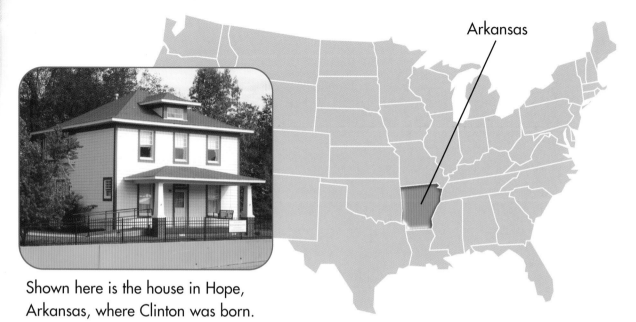

Arkansas

Shown here is the house in Hope, Arkansas, where Clinton was born.

Map of the United States of America

When Bill Clinton first ran for president, in 1992, he said, "I still believe in a place called Hope." Clinton had spent the first four years of his life in a town called Hope, Arkansas. His grandparents, James Eldridge Cassidy and Edith Grisham Cassidy, raised him there while his mother attended nursing school. In 1995, the two-story wood-frame house the family lived in was made to look as it did when Clinton was a young boy. Today the house belongs to the Clinton Birthplace Foundation. On display are photographs and Clinton memorabilia, or objects related to President Clinton's life. The house is on the National Register of Historic Places.

Clinton began his political career in Little Rock, the capital of Arkansas. He served two years as state attorney general and five terms as governor of Arkansas. In November 2004, President Clinton helped open the Clinton Presidential Library on the Arkansas River in Little Rock. The library holds photographs and documents from Clinton's life and political career. On display at the library are a collection of Clinton's saxophones and a large model of the Oval Office.

The Clinton Presidential Library was built on 27 acres (11 ha) of land on the south bank of the Arkansas River. The library has more than 1.8 million photos and 77 million documents.

Clinton's Youth

Bill Clinton was born in Hope, Arkansas, on August 19, 1946. As a young child, he spent a great deal of time with his grandparents. Although they had little education, James Eldridge Cassidy and Edith Cassidy taught their grandson to read and count by the time he was three years old. When he was seven years old, Bill moved with his mother and stepfather to Hot Springs, Arkansas.

At Hot Springs High School, Clinton was junior-class president and performed in the junior-class play. He also played the tenor saxophone in the marching band, concert band, and in a jazz band called the 3 Kings. In 1963, Bill attended the Boys Nation program in Washington, D.C., at which students from around the country studied politics and held mock elections. On a visit to the White House with the program, shown above, Bill met President John F. Kennedy.

1

The saxophone shown on page 10 is like the one Bill Clinton played when he was in school. Begin your drawing of the saxophone by making a tall rectangular guide.

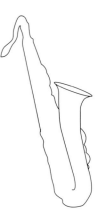

2

Draw two long slanted lines inside the rectangular guide. Add six shorter slanted lines and two short horizontal lines as shown. The part of the saxophone on the far left is the mouthpiece.

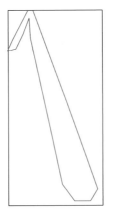

3

Use slanted lines and a curved line to finish drawing the guides for the saxophone. Start by drawing the short slanted lines at the top of the right side of the saxophone. This part of the instrument is called the bell.

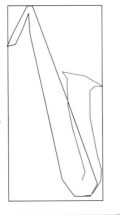

4

Using the guides you drew in step 2 and step 3, draw the outline of the saxophone. Remember to make the bumps outside of the guide on the left side of the saxophone.

5

Erase all the guides, including the rectangular guide from step 1.

6

Draw 19 curved lines on the saxophone as shown. Add the slanted line and two horizontal lines near the bottom. Draw eight ovals and six curved shapes as shown. Then draw wavy lines as shown.

7

Add nine curved lines to the saxophone as shown. Then add three wavy lines as shown.

8

Finish your drawing with shading. The mouthpiece is the darkest part.

The College Years

In fall 1964, Bill Clinton moved to Washington, D.C., to attend the Georgetown University School of Foreign Service. He chose the school because he wanted to live in the nation's capital and learn how the federal government was run. Clinton was elected class president during his first two years at Georgetown. During his third year, he took a part-time job working for Arkansas senator J. William Fulbright as an assistant clerk for the Foreign Relations Committee.

In April 1968, the civil rights leader Martin Luther King Jr. was murdered in Tennessee. The shock of his death set off national riots. Clinton witnessed the riots in Washington, D.C., and later helped give out food and blankets to families whose homes had been destroyed.

After graduating from Georgetown in 1968, Clinton won a scholarship that pays for promising students to attend Oxford University in England. He spent two years there studying politics and traveling around Europe. The university's crest is shown above.

1

On page 12, you can see the crest of University College at Oxford University, where Clinton was a student. A crest is a picture that stands for a family or place. Begin your drawing of the crest with a rectangle.

2

Inside the rectangle from step 1 draw two smaller rectangles as shown.

3

Draw another rectangle inside the three rectangles from step 2. Add slanted lines connecting the corners of the four rectangles as shown.

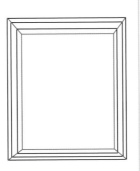

4

Draw a horizontal line. Add two lines that curve and meet at a point below the horizontal line as shown.

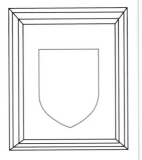

5

Add four horizontal lines and four vertical lines as shown. The lines should make a cross shape. Add four squiggly lines to make the ends of the cross. Each end should have three bumps.

6

Look carefully at the drawing and then use wavy lines to draw the four birds as shown.

7

Look carefully at the drawing. Draw the curling shapes around the shield. Start with the shapes on top. Then add the shapes to the left, at the bottom, and to the right.

8

Shade in your picture of the University College crest. You can leave the cross and the birds blank.

The Professor and Politics

After returning from England in 1970, Bill Clinton went to law school at Yale University in Connecticut. While at Yale he worked for George McGovern's presidential campaign and attended the Democratic National Convention in Florida. A national convention is the event at which a political party officially selects its candidate for president. After graduating from Yale, Clinton got a job as an assistant professor at the University of Arkansas Law School in Fayetteville, Arkansas.

In winter 1974, Clinton ran for Congress in Arkansas. To win votes Clinton traveled and spoke to voters throughout the 21 counties in his district. This district, the northwest part of Arkansas, included the mountainous regions of the Ozarks and Ouachita mountains, as well as the Arkansas River valley. Despite his efforts Clinton lost the race to the congressman, John Paul Hammerschmidt. In January 1975, Clinton went back to teaching.

1

The picture on the facing page shows a pin from McGovern's 1972 presidential campaign. Begin your drawing of the McGovern pin by making a square. It will serve as a guide for your drawing.

2

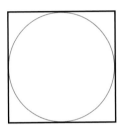

Draw a circle inside the square guide from step 1. It should touch each of the square's four sides.

3

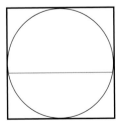

Draw a horizontal line inside the circle from step 2. It should be a little below the middle of the circle.

4

Erase the square guide. Write a large, open M above the line as shown. Add the letters G-O-V-E-R-N next to the M. Above that add the letter C and a star as shown.

5

Write "FOR PRESIDENT" in open letters below the line. Add "1972" below that. Draw two slanted lines for the end of the pin sticking out below the circle.

6

Finish your drawing of the McGovern pin with shading. The background of the top part of the pin should be shaded. The words on the bottom half of the pin should also be shaded.

Hillary Rodham Clinton

On October 11, 1975, Bill Clinton married Hillary Rodham in Fayetteville, Arkansas. The two had met as law students at Yale. There Rodham helped edit the Yale Law Review, a paper that explores matters of law. She was born in Chicago, Illinois, on October 26, 1947, and had attended Wellesley College in Massachusetts. When Clinton became president, she became one of his political advisers. In his first term, President Clinton selected Hillary to head the Health Care Task Force, a project aimed at providing health insurance, or money to cover medical costs. The proposal failed to pass in Congress. Hillary Clinton has continued working for increased health-care coverage for Americans.

On November 7, 2000, New York elected Hillary Clinton to the U.S. Senate. The Senate forms committees to address different tasks. Hillary Clinton has served on several committees, including the Health, Education, Labor, and Pensions Committee.

1

The picture of Hillary Rodham Clinton on page 16 was taken in 1969. At that time she was a student at Wellesley College. Begin your drawing of her with a rectangular guide.

2

Draw an oval for her head. Add eight slanted lines to make a guide for her body. Add more slanted lines as shown to make guides for her arms and her hands.

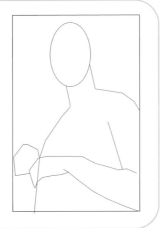

3

Add three circles and a curved line as guides for her eyes, her nose, and her mouth. Use wavy lines to draw the shapes of her face and hair. Use more wavy lines to draw her arms and hands as shown.

4

Use the guides from step 3 to draw her eyes, her eyebrows, her nose, and her mouth. Add small wavy lines to her face as shown. Add wavy lines for the waves in her hair.

5

Erase all extra lines, including the rectangular guide from step 1.

6

Add slightly curved lines for the edge of her sleeve and her arm below the sleeve. Add wavy lines for the top and the side of her sleeve. Add more wavy lines for the folds in her clothes.

7

Draw ovals and lines as shown for her necklace.

8

Now you are ready to shade in your drawing of Hillary Rodham Clinton. The darkest parts are her mouth, her eyes, and her eyebrows.

17

Governor of Arkansas

In 1976, Bill Clinton successfully ran for state attorney general of Arkansas. The attorney general is the state's top law officer and represents the state government on legal issues. Clinton served two years in this post. In 1978, Clinton ran for governor of Arkansas and won the election. He took office in January 1979, at the age of 32. During his first term, Governor Clinton passed state laws that raised education funding by 40 percent. He also tried to improve Arkansas's health-care system, repair state highways and roads, and encourage people to save energy.

On February 27, 1980, the Clintons' daughter, Chelsea, was born. The family lived in the governor's house in Little Rock. Clinton often arranged to work from home so that he could be near his daughter. The following fall Clinton lost his bid for reelection. However, two years later he ran again and won.

1

The top picture on page 18 shows the Arkansas state capitol in Little Rock, Arkansas. Begin your drawing of the capitol building by making a tall rectangular guide.

2

Draw a rectangle inside the rectangular guide. Add two horizontal lines to the right of the rectangle and two horizontal lines to the left. Add two vertical lines and a horizontal line above the rectangle.

3

Look carefully at the drawing. Draw curved lines to make the dome and the area below it, called the rotunda. Draw the columns and small dome on top of the big dome.

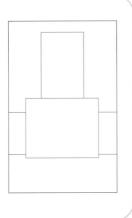

4 Draw curved lines and a triangle below the rotunda. Add horizontal, vertical, and slanted lines to make the shape below the triangle. Add more horizontal, vertical, and slanted lines to make the shapes on the building's sides.

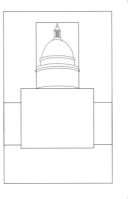

5

Draw two curved lines and 20 vertical lines to make the columns of the rotunda. Add slanted and horizontal lines to the main part of the building as shown.

6

Add a rectangle to the front of the building. Draw six vertical lines and a horizontal line inside it as shown. Add four vertical lines to the building's sides. Add 11 rectangular windows and two circular windows.

7

Use squiggly lines to draw the two rows of trees and the bushes behind them. Add trunks to the trees. Draw a curved shape with a thin pointed shape above it for the flagpole between the rows of trees.

8

Finish your drawing with shading. Notice where the shading is darker in some parts.

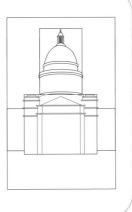

Running for President

In 1990, Bill Clinton ran for a fifth term as governor of Arkansas. He told the people of his state that he would finish his term. However, as the Democratic presidential primaries approached, Clinton began to consider running for U.S. president. He therefore asked the people of Arkansas if they would free him from his promise.

On October 3, 1991, Clinton announced his decision to run as the Democratic candidate for president of the United States. On July 8, he asked Albert Gore Jr., a senator from Tennessee, to be his running mate, or the candidate for vice president. Clinton ran against the Republican president, George H. W. Bush, and a Texan businessman named H. Ross Perot. In his campaign Clinton promised to overhaul the health, welfare, and education systems, while reducing the federal deficit. Clinton won with 43 percent of the popular vote, which is the total number of votes that a candidate receives throughout the country.

1

Clinton and Gore used the bus shown on page 20 during the 1992 presidential campaign. Begin your drawing of Clinton's campaign bus by making a long rectangle. It will be the guide for your drawing.

 5

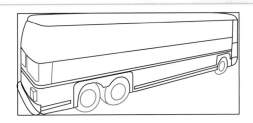

Use ovals and curved lines to draw the tires. Look carefully at the drawing. Draw the shape at the bottom of the back of the bus. Add slanted and vertical lines as shown.

2

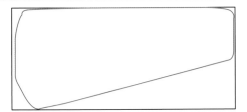

Look carefully at the drawing. Then use the rectangular guide to draw the outline of the bus.

6

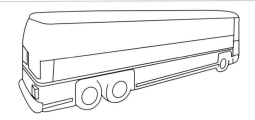

Erase all extra lines, including the rectangular guide from step 1.

 3

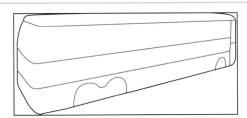

Draw a vertical line in the left part of the shape from step 1. Add a short slanted line. Draw three long slanted lines that curve at the back of the bus. Draw holes for the tires along the bottom of the bus.

 7

Add ovals to the middle of each of the three wheels. Write "Clinton / Gore '92" on the side of the bus. You can leave a bit of space between "Gore" and "'92."

 4

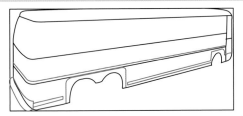

Erase any extra lines. Draw lines around the tire holes as shown. Add two slanted lines and a short vertical line to the bottom of the bus. Draw the two shapes at the back of the bus. Draw a line along the side of the bus.

 8

Shade in your drawing of the campaign bus. The tires and the writing should be the darkest parts.

The First Term

Bill Clinton signed his first bill into law on February 5, 1993. This was the Family and Medical Leave Act, which secured American workers three months off to care for newborn babies or sick family members. Clinton also helped pass the North American Free Trade Agreement, called NAFTA, in 1993. The NAFTA flag is shown here. NAFTA made trade easier between the United States, Canada, and Mexico by slowly removing tariffs among them and freeing their businesses from some local, state, and national regulations. Some Americans were concerned that NAFTA would lower workers' wages and destroy many American jobs if goods could be made more cheaply in Mexico or Canada.

On August 22, 1996, Clinton signed a bill into law that set five-year time limits on welfare benefits and required people receiving aid to find jobs within two years. At the same time, more financial aid was given to day care and health-care programs. Such aid would make it easier for poor people with children to work.

1

The flag on page 20 stands for NAFTA. The NAFTA flag is made of parts of the American, Mexican, and Canadian flags. It stands for the three countries working together. Begin your drawing of the flag with a rectangle.

2

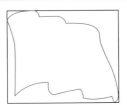

Look carefully at the drawing. Draw the outline of the flag. Start with the sides of the flag. Then draw the top and the bottom.

3

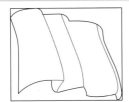

Draw three wavy lines that go from the top to the bottom of the flag. Add a slightly curved line near the bottom of the flag as shown.

4

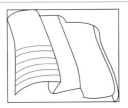

Draw six curved lines for the stripes on the left side of the flag. The left side of the flag comes from the American flag.

5

Draw the shape on the right side of the flag. Look carefully at the drawing for help. The shape is a maple leaf. It comes from the Canadian flag.

6

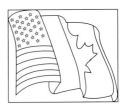

Look carefully at the drawing. Draw 27 stars on the left side of the flag as shown. The stars are lined up in six columns of four or five stars each.

7

Look carefully at the drawing. Draw the bird in the middle of the flag. The bird is an eagle. Draw the shape below the eagle. It is a cactus on which the eagle is resting. The eagle and the cactus come from the Mexican flag.

8

Finish your drawing of the NAFTA flag with shading. You can leave the parts of the flag that are supposed to be white blank.

The Second Term

Bill Clinton ran for reelection in 1996. Americans were happy with the economy, and Clinton was reelected. One of Clinton's goals for his second term was to address the nation's finances. When Clinton first took office, the federal budget deficit was $290 billion. By reducing the deficit, the government could spend more money on its citizens, rather than paying interest on the money it borrowed. In 1997, Clinton passed the Balanced Budget Act, which created a surplus of $236 billion by 2000.

In his final year as president, Clinton continued his efforts to bring peace to the Middle East. In January 2000, he hosted peace talks in West Virginia between Israel and Syria over the fate of the Golan Heights, a strip of land on the Sea of Galilee. The Golan Heights, which was originally a part of Syria, had been occupied by Israel in 1967. Unfortunately, no agreement was reached.

1

The map on page 24 shows the Middle East. To begin your own map of the Middle Eastern countries of Israel and Syria, draw a large rectangle. The rectangle is almost a square. However, it is a little longer than it is high.

2

Look carefully at the drawing. Notice how the shape fits into the rectangular guide. Use slanted lines to draw a guide for the outline of the two countries.

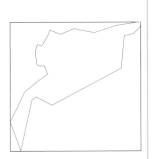

3

Use the guide you drew in step 2 to draw the outline of Syria and Israel. Look carefully at the drawing for help.

4

Erase all the guides from step 1 and step 2.

5

Add five squiggly lines. The bottom two lines show the Gaza Strip and the West Bank. They are areas that Israel controlled in 2000. The line above the West Bank shows the border between Israel and Syria. The line to the right is the Orontes River. The Euphrates River is farther right.

6

Finish your map with shading. Shade in Israel darker so that you can see which country is which.

Clinton and the Environment

Caring for the environment was an important issue to President Clinton. In his first term, he supported the Safe Drinking Water Act, the Clean Water Act, as well as improvements to the Superfund Program, which aimed to clean up polluted places that had been abandoned.

Over the course of his two terms, Clinton brought a total of 5.6 million acres (2.3 million ha) of land under federal protection by making them national monuments. This protection banned or limited the use of cars or trucks, mining, and oil drilling from these locations. In June 2000, Clinton set aside land for national monuments in Arizona, Colorado, Oregon, and Washington. One piece of the land that Clinton set aside was the Ironwood Forest National Monument. Located in the Sonoran Desert in Arizona, the Ironwood Forest National Monument provides a natural home for bighorn sheep, desert tortoises, gila monsters, and an endangered species called the lesser long-nosed bat.

1

The cactus on page 26 is a saguaro cactus from Ironwood Forest National Monument. The saguaro cactus is the biggest kind of cactus that grows in the United States. Begin your drawing of the cactus with a rectangular guide.

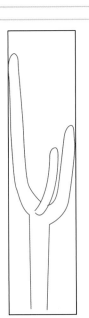

2

Draw two slanted lines for the bottom of the cactus. Use a long wavy line to draw the tall arm of the cactus on the left. Draw the arm of the cactus on the right. Add the arm in the middle.

3

Look carefully at the drawing. Add two smaller arms to the cactus's left arm and one smaller arm to its right arm. Finish drawing the trunk. This is the tall part in the middle. Remember to draw the arms growing on the trunk as well.

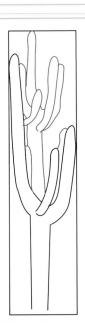

4

Erase the rectangular guide that you drew in step 1.

5

Use zigzag lines to draw the grass below the cactus.

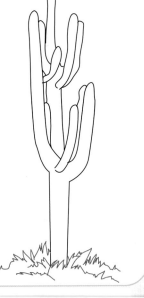

6

Shade in your drawing of the saguaro cactus. Notice that some of the arms are darker than others.

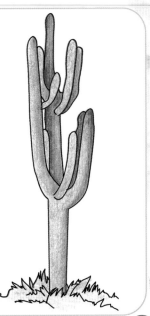

After the Presidency

After leaving office in January 2001, Bill Clinton moved to New York, where Hillary Rodham Clinton was a senator. He opened an office in the Harlem neighborhood of New York City and formed the Clinton Foundation. It is an organization that works on global economic, social, and health issues. Clinton also spent time writing. In June 2004, he published a personal account of his life, called *My Life*.

Clinton has also worked in Africa and Asia to call attention to deadly sicknesses, such as AIDS. After a terrible tsunami struck countries around the Indian Ocean in December 2004, Clinton traveled to the areas that were harmed.

As president Bill Clinton was known for his ability to relate to the people he met and to show them that he cared about their troubles. This quality has continued to serve him in his other ventures.

1

The picture of President William Jefferson Clinton on page 28 was taken in 1997. This was during Clinton's second term as president. Begin your drawing of Clinton by making a tall rectangular guide.

2

Draw an oval as a guide for his head. Use slanted lines to make guides for his body and his hands. Add more slanted lines to make guides for the edges of his shirt and his jacket.

3

Draw three circles and a slanted line as guides for his eyes, his nose, and his mouth. Draw wavy lines for his face, his neck, his ear, and his hands. Use squiggly lines for his hair and the inside of his ear.

4

Use wavy lines to draw the arms and shoulders of his jacket. Use curved lines to draw his tie, the edges of his jacket, and the collar of his shirt.

5

Look closely at the drawing. Use the guides from step 3 to draw his eyes, his nose, and his mouth. Draw his eyebrows. Add lines to his face as shown. Add wavy lines for the waves in his hair.

6

Erase all the guides from the earlier steps, including the rectangular guide from step 1.

7

Use curved and slanted lines to draw the collar of his jacket as shown. Add wavy lines for the folds in his jacket. Draw a trapezoid that is almost a square and two wavy lines to make his watch.

8

You can now shade in your drawing of President Clinton. His watch and his jacket should be the darkest parts.

Timeline

1946 William Jefferson Clinton is born on August 19.

1964 Bill Clinton graduates from Hot Springs High School.

1968 Bill Clinton graduates from Georgetown University in Washington, D.C., and goes to Oxford University in England on a Rhodes Scholarship.

1973 Clinton graduates from law school at Yale University in Connecticut.

1974 Clinton runs for Congress but loses.

1975 Clinton marries Hillary Rodham on October 11.

1976 Clinton is elected attorney general of Arkansas.

1978 Clinton is elected governor of Arkansas.

1982–1992 Clinton is reelected four times as governor of Arkansas.

1993 Clinton takes office as U.S. president. Clinton passes the Family and Medical Leave Act and NAFTA.

1996 Clinton is reelected as president of the United States.

1997 Clinton passes the Balanced Budget Act.

2000 Clinton hosts peace talks in West Virginia between Israel and Syria and a meeting at Camp David between Israel and Palestine.

2001 Clinton moves to New York.

2004 Clinton opens the Clinton Presidential Library and publishes *My Life*.

2005 The United Nations names Clinton special envoy, or special representative, for tsunami recovery.

Glossary

access (AK-ses) A way to get something easily.

billion (BIL-yun) One thousand millions.

civil rights movement (SIH-vul RYTS MOOV-mint) People and groups working together to win freedom and equality for all.

committee (kuh-MIH-tee) A group of people directed to consider a matter.

crust (KRUST) The outer, or top, layer of a planet.

deficit (DEH-fuh-sut) What results when more money has been spent than earned.

endangered species (in-DAYN-jerd SPEE-sheez) A kind of animal or plant that will probably die out if people do not protect it.

environment (en-VY-ern-ment) All the living things and conditions of a place.

foreign (FOR-in) Outside one's own country.

pensions (PEN-shunz) Money paid when people retire from a job.

primaries (PRY-mer-eez) Early elections in which a political party decides who will represent it in a larger election.

professor (preh-FEH-ser) A teacher at a college, or a school for advanced students.

regulations (reh-gyuh-LAY-shunz) Rules issued by an authority or government.

riots (RY-uts) Mass displays of disorderly and out-of-control conduct.

scholarship (SKAH-ler-ship) Money given to someone to pay for school.

segregated (SEH-gruh-gayt-ed) Separated by race.

surplus (SUR-plus) An amount of money that is more than what is needed.

tariffs (TER-ufs) Taxes on goods from another country.

tsunami (soo-NAH-mee) A series of waves caused by a movement in Earth's crust on the ocean floor.

welfare (WEL-fer) The money that is given to poor people so they can improve their living conditions.

Index

Web Sites

Due to the changing nature of Internet links, PowerKids Press has developed an online list of Web sites related to the subject of this book. This site is updated regularly. Please use this link to access the list:
www.powerkidslinks.com/kgdpusa/clinton/